AF351856

Grow Your Glow: An Art Therapy & Writing Prompt Journal for Self-Love.
Stephanie McLeod-Estevez, MA, LCPC, Author.
Designed by Stephanie McLeod-Estevez.
Interior artwork by Stephanie McLeod-Estevez.
www.stephaniemcleodestevez.com

Copyright © 2025 by Creative Transformations, LLC.
Library of Congress Cataloging-in-Publication Data has been applied for.

All rights reserved. Printed in the United States of America. No part of this book may be reproduced, scanned, or distributed in any manner whatsoever without written permission from the publisher except for the inclusion of brief excerpts or quotations embodied in critical articles or reviews.

First Edition. ISBN 979-8-9941640-0-6

Published by Creative Transformations, LLC
P.O. Box 734
Westbrook, ME 04098

GROW YOUR GLOW

An Art Therapy & Writing Prompt Journal for Self-Love

Stephanie McLeod-Estévez, LCPC

Art Therapist, Host of the *Live Radiantly Talk Show*

Name: _______________________________

Email: _______________________________

Phone: _______________________________

*This book is dedicated to all of the souls who know, deep down, they are worthy.
I see you, thank you for seeing me.*

Self-love may feel elusive—but it already lives within you.

Using art therapy and writing, you'll learn how to connect with and feel the energy of love that is patiently waiting for you inside.

The exercises are designed to spark your curiosity and creativity. Both are powerful allies that know you're worthy of this journey. The prompts encourage you to be playful and soulful so that you can engage with your highest vibration, your self-love.

These small steps appear deceptively simple, yet they yield big rewards. You'll be surprised by how effective combining art therapy with writing can be for healing and growth.

You'll experience how regenerative self-love is. It's a wellspring of renewal that replenishes, revitalizes, and strengthens your unique life force. This is energy of your soul that wants to nourish you from the inside out. It's how you can move from surviving to thriving, which will ripple out into the world around you.

As a personal commitment to the power of love, I will donate quarterly at least 5% of the profits from this book and its workshops to life-affirming nonprofits that support social justice, medical research, environmental care, and humanitarian aid. Thank you for your contribution!

This journal is both a personal companion and a shared journey. May it guide you back to your inner glow and remind you of the love that has always been yours.

In Solidarity,

Stephanie

PS. You do not need to be an artist to do art therapy. This guided journal will walk you through the process, with the information you need to know and tips that will get you there!

"Every creative act brings something to life."

Hello! I'm Stephanie. Your guide through the self-love journey you're about to embark upon...

The wisdom and exercises within this journal are the culmination of my life's work as an art therapist—woven together with the insight I've gained from my lived experience of healing from childhood trauma, significant loss, and surviving an aggressive form of breast cancer when I was 40.

Through it all, I've learned the immeasurable value of going inward and cultivating a powerful relationship with myself. Life's hardships brought me a lot of lessons related to self-worth, but deep inside I've always felt a warm glow that encouraged me to keep the faith.

Even when that inner light felt dimmed, it was never extinguished. I persisted because I knew I was here for a reason. This guided journal reflects my determination, what I lovingly call my sacred stubbornness, to walk the path of healing and growth despite the obstacles I've faced.

When my cancer treatment ended, I realized more than ever how precious life is. I knew I wanted to honor this gift of time.

I made a commitment to live my life as well as I could, which meant attending to the needs of my body, mind, spirit, and self. Over time, this effort blossomed into a deep self-love I never could have imagined or predicted was possible.

Through art therapy, writing, and genuine self-acceptance, I discovered what it truly means to live radiantly.

This helped me understand my purpose, to share what I've learned and created, so that we can all shine. For it is through our light that we can embody self-love and serve the greater good of all.

Thank you for joining me on this journey!

From my heart to yours,

Stephanie

**These exercises are just the beginning.
May they spark your light, help you embrace your glow,
and guide you to love yourself from the inside out.**

Table of Contents

Table of Contents

How to Use this Book

It's my intention that you have what you need to successfully use this journal. Here's how to embark upon that journey, whether you're an art therapy novice or an art making muse, someone who's used it for a long time.

Feel inspired by the intention and magic of this journal by reading about The 4 Pillars and The Show and Tell Method.

Then benefit from the guidance offered in these sections: Intro to Art Therapy, Intro to Therapeutic Writing, Suggested Supplies, Art Therapy Warm Up, and How to Use the Prompts. Plus, I've given you a personal example and two YouTube videos that walk you through the warm up and my process of working with one of the prompts. This guidance will lessen the performance anxiety you feel and help you understand how to get the most out of the art therapy and writing prompts. Additional tips are offered throughout the book, see the list on page 8.

Then you'll be ready to get started. The guided prompts are divided into four sections: body, mind, spirit, and self. Each section has five unique prompts for you to try. You get to decide whether or not it feels best to focus on one area at a time, or move between the four. Trust your instinct as to what feels right.

Select a prompt for your journey and set up your art supplies. Spend 5-10 minutes focusing on each prompt by immersing yourself in the visualization. Then use the Show & Tell Method to reflect what happened so you can grow your glow!

Did you know?

When you move from making art to writing, you can:

- tap into different parts of your brain by shifting the form of creative expression. This helps you process your feelings more deeply;

- increase self-awareness and understanding of how your experiences have impacted you;

- move more easily through creative blocks;

- and release the tension that you've held onto.

In art therapy, we call this process of moving from one form of expression to another an intermodal transfer.

The Four Pillars of Self-Love: Body, Mind, Spirit, and Self

There's this song I used to sing as a kid that has this line in it: "You can't have one without the other". It's a line from a Frank Sinatra song called "Love and Marriage".

As a highly sensitive child, every time I sang these words, I felt them deep in my core. I couldn't quite name it at the time, but on some level, I understood that these words were talking about the power of love and acceptance.

One of the reasons why self-love can feel so elusive is it challenges you to recognize that you can't truly love yourself if there are parts of yourself you reject. These parts usually bring up feelings of shame, guilt, and judgment when you think about them. But in reality, they represent what you need to work though for healing and growth.

Cancer taught me the importance of focusing on influence, not control. As scary as it was to give up my desire to control, it was also incredibly liberating. I realized that if I was going to reclaim my life, I needed to start small, because the enormity of what I was undertaking could easily overwhelm me.

This is where the 4 pillars of self-love come into play.

By dividing the work into these four pillars, I gave myself permission to see what was needed, right here, right now. This focus helped me to chip away and discern where I had influence over my health and wellbeing.

The Four Pillars of Self-Love: Body, Mind, Spirit, and Self

When you work with the 4 pillars, you discover new pathways to feel self-love. Each area offers lessons and wisdom that will help you grow your self-love glow.

Your body is a lifelong relationship that represents love at a cellular level.

Your mind is a center of wisdom and intuition when powered by love.

Your spirit is your unique radiance. It's where your purpose, possibilities, and guiding light lives, helping you through the highs and lows of life.

Your self is the center of connection between your pillars. It reflects how your story crafts your identity and builds your resilience for navigating life.

Life always serves us lessons we didn't plan for. This is why working on your self-love is so important. It can give you the perseverance you need to deal with whatever curveballs life throws at you.

What's remarkable about going down this path of radical self-acceptance is the unburdening that can happen. When you practice genuine self-love and acceptance, you reclaim your energy for the personal transformation that lies ahead.

The good news is that you do not need to take on drastic change to get the ball rolling with self-love. You just need to find a place to begin. **This is why *Grow Your Glow* is a prompt-driven journal, so you can take one step at a time towards loving yourself.**

The Show & Tell Method

I don't know about you, but I loved Show and Tell when I was a child. Each week I felt anticipation for the moment in which I got to share a favorite toy and tell why it meant so much to me. And then, I got to experience the magic of feeling connected to others by hearing about the treasures my classmates had to share.

Show and Tell helped me create joy inside. It was also a valuable way for me to proclaim, without hesitation, this is who I am. A powerful affirmation of my pure self-acceptance and self-love.

As an art therapist, now I know that Show and Tell revealed two important ingredients for generating self-love. These ingredients are playfulness and soulfulness.

No matter how old you are, you benefit from the lightness and spontaneity of play. This version of love encourages you to find the whimsy, the ease of feeling joy in the smallest aspects of yourself and life. This helps you shake the heaviness that masks your glow without having to force it.

The Show & Tell Method inside of *Grow your Glow* gives you the opportunity to heal and grow through the power of play.

Soulfulness represents how profound love can be. The kind of energy that connects you deeply to yourself. Soulfulness feeds your inner glow, your self-love, so that you can rely upon the deep reservoir of resilience you have within.

The Show & Tell Method

The Show & Tell Method inside of *Grow your Glow* gives you the opportunity to feel, replenish, and strengthen your unique soulfulness.

The other reason why the Show & Tell Method is a critical component for *Grow Your Glow* is that the magic of art therapy lies not only in creating something, but in the describing of what you did. Here's why.

When you show how you feel inside using your art supplies, you proclaim that you matter. This demonstrates a willingness to care for yourself and validate your experience. This humble act can shift everything.

When you tell, or describe, what your drawing, painting, or collage represents, you deepen your understanding. Writing illuminates what your unconscious has shown you through the art. By taking the time to describe your creation, you find the words that reflect the wisdom of your unconscious.

When you bring this insight into consciousness, you feel greater affirmation and understanding. This enhances creative problem solving and strengthens your sense of self.

This is why *Grow Your Glow* includes both. Art therapy and writing take you further along the path of self-love than intention alone. The Show & Tell Method helps you embrace the fullness of self-love through experiencing it in your body, mind, spirit, and self.

Intro to Art Therapy

Art therapy is a form of communication.

- It tells your story through color, shape, & form.
- It enables your conscious and unconscious mind to communicate with one another.
- It can help you see how you feel, this visibility can help you understand yourself better and find creative solutions.
- This helps you express the energy inside that words alone often fail to capture.
- Art therapy feels like resonance, the feeling of being understood by the most important person in your life... yourself.

When you art-it-out, you use your art supplies to represent all of your thoughts, feelings, and beliefs without judgment or trying to force yourself to feel better and more positive. You're actively practicing self-acceptance, a crucial component for healing and growth.

When you art-it-in, you use your art supplies to reflect what you need. For example, you might visually represent what self-love and self-care feels like when you experience it with your thoughts, feelings, and in your energy. By representing your supportive reply through art, you grow your glow, one step at a time.

Art therapy can feel magical.

It helps you tap into your E.S.P., an acronym I developed to explain how art therapy makes you feel.

- **E stands for Express**: by showing how you feel on the inside, you reap the reward of full expression of your experience. This helps you release what you've held onto. It also supports your ability to embody your thoughts, feelings and sensations more fully.

- **S stands for Soothe**: the energetic response you feel inside when you feel seen and heard. You feel peaceful even when you've leaned into something painful. This allows your nervous system to relax.

- **P stands for Process**: when you've fully expressed yourself, when you feel soothed by feeling validated, you get to the most juicy part, understanding yourself better. Being able to process your experiences helps you to discover creative solutions, make meaning from your experiences, and find purpose. This helps you communicate and share your experience with greater ease.

When you practice E.S.P. together, your glow naturally grows.

Intro to Therapeutic Writing

Therapeutic writing helps you clarify how you feel.

- It helps you find your words. Seeing how you feel through art and then describing it through writing will enhance your self-awareness and understanding. You feel more confident when you can articulate what words alone could not capture.
- It assists you in connecting with your subconscious. This can illuminate aspects of yourself and your artwork that you weren't aware of before.
- Therapeutic writing supports your ability to work with limiting beliefs by exposing them, increasing your understanding of their impact, and providing the opportunity to re-write them to benefit your healing and growth.
- The insight you gain from adding therapeutic writing to art therapy makes it easier to share your experience with others. This can improve your communication skills and deepen your relationships.

Listen to your instinct about what type of writing you wish to do with each prompt. You could choose to write in story form, word collage, poetry, prose, or even as a letter. There's no right or wrong way to do it, so tune into what feels right to you.

Writing Tips

It's recommended that you use free writing on the TELL pages of *Grow Your Glow.*

This is a form of writing without stopping, without paying attention to spelling and punctuation. It's about trying to capture any and all thoughts, words, feelings, etc. that are surfacing from the conscious and unconscious mind.

Your free writing is meant to describe what your artwork reflects about each prompt in the journal. Here are a few questions you can use to kick off your free-write.

- What are the words that come to mind when you look at what you created?
- What do the colors and shapes represent your experience?
- How would you describe it to someone else?
- If your artwork could speak, what would it say?
- If you were to give your work a title, what would it be?

Pro Tip: You may want to free write on a separate page if you'd like to create a poem, letter, story, etc. You can circle the words that are calling your attention and then use them to create the final written piece in your *Grow Your Glow* journal.

Suggested Supplies

When choosing your art supplies, it's important to be mindful of what your comfort level is with art therapy. Especially in the beginning, you might want to start with what feels really familiar to you. This will help lessen any performance anxiety that might come up.

At the same time, this is also meant to be fun. So if there's an art medium you are craving to work with, trust your instinct!

You can use any medium (pencil, paint, etc.) and any form of creating (like drawing, painting, or collaging) that suits your comfort level, preference, and personality to do the *Grow Your Glow* Prompts.

The following supplies are what I recommend having available. You do not need to have them all. It's helpful to have a mix of supplies to be able to fully express yourself with art therapy, including ones that are easier to control, like pencils, and ones you can blend easily, like oil or chalk pastels.

Start with the basics:
- Pens & pencils
- Colored pencils/watercolor pencils and/or markers
- Collage material, glue sticks, Modge Podge
- Wax paper and/or adhesive spray to protect and limit smudging from pastels

Select at least 1 blend-able medium for more variety:
- Oil and/or chalk pastels (oil pastels are sometimes labeled craypas)
- Charcoal sticks
- Watercolor or Acrylic paint set, brushes, and a paint pallet (needed for tube-style watercolors and acrylic paints)

Set Yourself Up for Success

Create the conditions that help you open up your creative instinct:

- **#1 Devise a welcoming environment**, set yourself up for making art like your best friend is coming over. This kind of intention says that you matter, reinforcing that this practice is an act of self-love and self-care.

- **#2 Put on music** that moves you to feel more connected and aware of yourself. Music can:
    - Match the tone of how you are feeling, which is affirming;
    - Invite greater flow with your creative expression;
    - Lift your spirits when you feel doubt;
    - Help you focus and trust the process.

- **#3 Light candles.** This enhances the spiritual aspects of art therapy: self-care and self-exploration. It's also warm and inviting, signaling that you're safe here.

Remember, focus on the process, not the outcome. The goal is self-expression and mental well-being, not a masterpiece. There are several art therapy tips to support you in this journal. Check out the Table of Contents to see the complete list.

The Art Therapy Warm-Up

Just like you do in a group fitness class, a warm-up helps you get ready for the work ahead. The art therapy warm-up serves the same purpose. It helps you feel less anxious about doing art therapy AND it helps you practice how to translate your feelings and energy through color, shape, and form.

As you draw, notice how you feel, this will help you translate your experience. A friendly reminder- there's no right or wrong way to do this!

Follow the instructions below to guide yourself through the warm-up, or follow along with me on YouTube. The QR Code and web address is below.

- Begin by making light marks on the paper. How gentle can you be and yet still create something, any kind of mark will do... What matters is that the mark is soft and gentle. As you do this, how do you feel inside? Tune in as you create these gentle... soft... light marks... trust whatever is coming up for you. What kinds of sensations... emotions... feelings are created with these light marks...

- Now, let's switch to pressing firmly onto the paper. How firm... strong... and sturdy can you be and yet still create something... As you do this, how does this make you feel inside? Tune in as you create these robust... solid... tenacious and firm marks... trust whatever is coming up for you. What kinds of sensations... emotions... feelings are created with these firm marks...

To access the YouTube Video, type:

https://youtu.be/GxrAkBNH5Mk or use this QR Code

The Art Therapy Warm-Up

- Now try moving slowly across the paper. How gradual and slow can you be and yet still create something... As you do this, how does this make you feel inside? Tune in as you create these gradual... unhurried... and slow marks... trust whatever is coming up for you. What kinds of sensations... emotions... and feelings are created with these slow marks...

- Now let's switch to moving quickly across your paper. Scribbling is welcome here. How swiftly... hastily... and fast can you be and yet still create something... As you do this, how does this make you feel inside? Tune in as you create these quick... fast... and hasty marks... trust whatever is coming up for you. What kinds of sensations... emotions... and feelings are created with these quick marks...

- Now let's make smooth shapes on the paper, like circles... ovals... spirals... shapes that do not have points on them. How smooth... effortless... and fluid can you and your shapes be? As you do this, how does this make you feel inside? Tune in as you create smooth shapes... trust whatever is coming up for you. What kinds of sensations... emotions... feelings are created with these smooth marks...

- Finally, let's make shapes with sharp edges on the paper, like triangles, zigzags, squares, and so forth... shapes that are pointy or have edges on them... How sharp and pointy can you and your shapes be? As you do this, how does this make you feel inside? Tune in as you create sharp shapes... trust whatever is coming up for you. What kinds of sensations... emotions... and feelings are created with these sharp marks...

You did it! Now it's time to begin.

How to Use the Prompts

A step-by-step guide:

- **Select a prompt that you would like to work with.** Reread the prompt multiple times to help you feel deeply connected to its message. Each one is designed to help you explore and experience self-love, with the understanding that incremental change can have a profound impact.

- **Then set a timer for 5 to 10 minutes.** Timers help you feel more safe and capable of surrendering to this practice, because you know that you'll be called back to the present when it goes off.

- **Soften or close your eyes.** Continue to focus on the message of the prompt until you notice that something is changing inside of you. You could experience this as:
    - feeling settled into the energy of the prompt;
    - seeing images that reflect the power of the prompt's impact;
    - noticing an intuitive, energetic shift, as if the prompt is like a medicine that helps your self-love grow;
    - or feeling an opening to what's possible when you love yourself.

Remember, there's no right or wrong way to experience these prompts. This is about trusting what happens and being open to the process of discovery. Use the art therapy warm up, as needed or desired, to help you feel more in touch with yourself. Prompts can be repeated.

How to Use the Prompts

When the timer has gone off and/or you feel a strong connection to your experience:

- **Open your eyes and use your art supplies to show what happened during the meditation.** If you are painting, put wax paper underneath the page to protect the other pages. Follow your creative instinct, even if it doesn't make sense to you at the time. Use color, shape, and form to represent your experience.

- **It's highly recommended that you follow this creative instinct for the entire time.** This is how you can benefit from the wisdom, healing, and growth that comes from your intuition.

- **When you feel unsure of what else is needed, talk to your creation, ask it what wants.** Create until you feel satisfied and complete.

- **Once you feel finished with your art supplies, it's time to write.** Describe what your creation reflects about your experience with the prompt you selected. Remember, you can always return to the Intro to Therapeutic Writing section for guidance.

You can learn more about art therapy, listen to my podcast, and **get access to audio recordings for the prompts in this book** when you sign up for my free Substack.
Visit www.stephaniemcleodestevez.com or use this QR code.

An Example of Using the Prompts

Using Prompt 4 from the Body Love Section

For a more detailed description of my work with this prompt, watch this YouTube Video. Type: https://youtu.be/9uOKKRRpusE or use this QR Code:

Describing What My Art Reflects

Using Prompt 4 from the Body Love Section

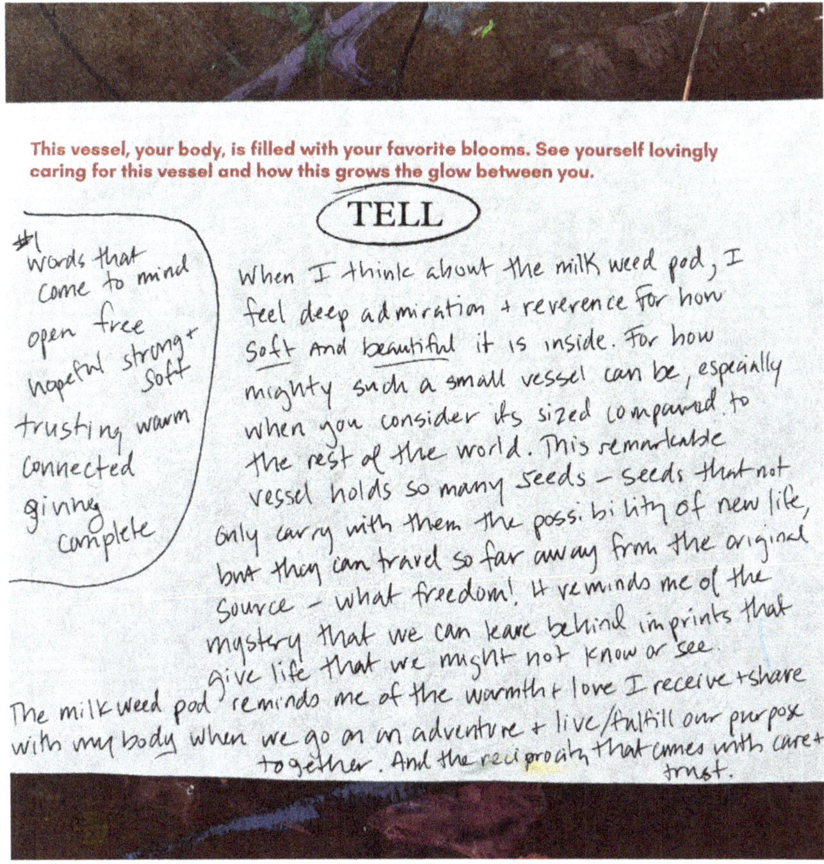

How did this prompt make me feel? So warm and beautiful.
The title I gave my creation?
What Living in Harmony with My Body Feels Like

BODY LOVE
PROMPTS

Let's nurture your relationship.

Your body is the most committed relationship you'll experience in your lifetime.

After all , it's been with you since the beginning. Even when your relationship with your body has been difficult, it does what it can to serve you.

Your body has been patiently waiting, holding space, and witnessing you through every aspect of your life. This vessel holds the raw rendition of your story, hoping for you to see it as an ally. Your body's honest revelations about your life can shake you to your core, but this clarity seeks to inspire you to heal, grow, and love yourself, fully and truly, from the inside out.

When you foster self-love and acceptance through the relationship with your body, it feels like coming home to yourself. Together, you can build a synergistic relationship that enhances your ability to influence your health and wellbeing.

SHOW IT THROUGH ART

your body like you would your favorite pet or animal. Experience how
you feel as you cherish your body in this way.

SHOW IT THROUGH ART

When you answer its call, see the glow from that cell spread throughout your entire body, filling you with love.

SHOW IT THROUGH ART

supports me, my body comforts me. My body is always by my side. Feel the power of radical acceptance and love between you and your body.

Prompt 4: Imagine your body as a beautiful vessel, one that tenderly holds you within its structure. This vessel, your body, is where your

SHOW IT THROUGH ART

life force and creative essence lives. See yourself lovingly caring for this vessel and how this grows the glow between you.

Prompt 5: Say to your body, in your head or out loud, "I love you, fully and truly, with every fiber of my being. I respect you, fully and truly,

SHOW IT THROUGH ART

deep in my bones. I honor you, fully and truly, with all my heart and soul." Notice how these words grow your connection and glow.

Myth Busting!

Only artists/creative people can benefit from art therapy.

This myth comes from memories of being criticized or judged for your unique creative voice when it didn't meet someone else's standards or expectations.

In my opinion, creativity is an innate gift every person has. Your creativity might look different from mine, but that doesn't make it any less valid.

In fact, reclaiming and rediscovering your unique creative voice is one way to feel empowered. It's my intention that by the time you complete this journal, you will have accomplished that fully and completely.

While it's normal to feel anxious about trying something new, keep in mind that the goal of using creativity for healing is not to create a masterpiece. The goal is to express your thoughts, feelings, and experiences using color, shape and form. Begin by asking yourself:

- What color matches my feelings?

- What marks or shapes reflect how my thoughts and emotions feel?

Trust what your instinct guides you to do when you start making art.
Remember to focus on the process, not the outcome, and before you know it you'll feel like you've moved from an art therapy novice to an art therapy muse.

Am I "doing it" right?

Figuring out whether or not you're "doing it" right with art therapy is a fair question to ask. Here are some cues that you can look for to help you affirm that yes, you are, indeed, "doing it" right:

- If you notice yourself feeling peaceful inside, you're doing it right. Because art therapy is all about being able to witness yourself and your experience. The #1 outcome I've noticed with myself and clients is that we feel "better... lighter... more clear" because the practice helps you feel validated by the most important person in your life- yourself.

- If you get lost in the creative process, you're doing it right. This is the flow state. You become absorbed by what you're doing that time just melts away, and often your tension and stress melts away too.

- If you start feeling an instinct of what you need to do with your art supplies and then decide to follow the guidance, even if it doesn't make sense to you at the time, you're doing it right. What do you get in return? Greater self awareness and understanding, unexpected resolutions and answers to the problems you're contending with, relief, celebration of your unique self, and more— and this begins by following your creative instinct.

MIND LOVE
PROMPTS

Let's nurture your relationship.

Your mind is the relationship between your brain and your gut. It holds your unique wisdom.

Your mind deeply influences how you perceive yourself, your circumstances, and the world around you. It can be an asset that helps you know what to do.

Yet, all too often, the healthy relationship you have with your mind is disrupted by experiences that you are still working through. Art therapy and writing can help you restore the communication loop between your analytical brain and your intuitive wisdom.

The greatest ah-ha moments come from your brain processing and releasing what no longer serves you and your gut instinct being able to tell you what feels right, even if it doesn't make sense at the time.

When you foster self-love and acceptance through the relationship with your mind, you release your need for control. This restores your mind's ability to guide you with love. May the following prompts help you feel this possibility.

SHOW IT THROUGH ART

Feel how this immersion of self-care brings a deep, calming release to your mind and how this grows the glow of love between you.

SHOW IT THROUGH ART

comes full circle. Imagine the water cleansing your brain and your gut, replenishing their energy. Feel the glow of love between you.

Appreciate what each has to offer. Listen to the intuitive wisdom that comes from nature for your mind's love to glow.

acceptance. Feel how your mind, when it is fueled by love, boosts your confidence and heals your relationship with one another.

Prompt 10: Imagine that your mind is being fed a beautiful meal that nourishes, heals, and soothes its tender spots and regenerates its

SHOW IT THROUGH ART

tissues. This meal is made of love and trust. See how this benefits your mind and adds to the glow of self-love within.

Neuroscience + Art Therapy

Art therapy benefits you by:

- **Regulating your emotions.** Art therapy helps you slow down through curiosity and observation. This relieves strong emotions and releases dopamine, AKA the "feel good" hormone.

- **Improving your neuroplasticity** (AKA mental flexibility). Art therapy bridges the unconscious and conscious mind, it improves your self-awareness and creative problem solving skills. This enables you to develop new coping strategies and behaviors that help you adapt to changes and challenges.

- **Enhancing your focus.** Art therapy helps externalize your thoughts, feelings and beliefs which settles your nervous system. This makes it easier to be in the present moment.

- **Activating your mirror neurons.** When active, your mirror neurons help you feel more empathy. This decreases the impact of the inner critic and improves your relationships (including the one you have with yourself).

11) Wake up at 5am daily to catch my most joyful alone time -as well as my inspired time
12) Abundance baby - financial, spiritual, love, time, inspiration with ease
13) Manifest regular 1:1 time with my kids + Justo
14) Staying calm or finding calm when I have to do something or accept something that interferes with my plan
15) More time with girlfriends
16) More time for writing, art making, + biz development/promotion
17) Family vacation with Matt + Donna + to Spain
18) An addition/remodelling of our home to make it more functional, more spacious, more comfy for guests + work, + address the concerns we have
19) a storage shed
20) gear 4 the car to do sports + camping more easily
21) outdoor fun gear for J+I - paddle bo - lakes
As Jupiter enters Pisces, I remind myself that the dreams I've tucked away, the dreams I've been too trepidatious to let into the light, dream about me too.
They want to love me
What is gestating has serious growth potential. The more I trust its development; the more I can supply it with what it needs next.
54

Art Therapy For Planting Seeds

Art therapy can help you pursue your intentions & goals by:

- **Creating a visual plan or map that helps guide your way.** Think of this as a vision board with a twist. How do your intentions and goals represent what you want for your body, mind, spirit, and self? Use art to reflect your replies.

- **Raising awareness of and working with feelings, thoughts, and beliefs that might be blocking your way.** Otherwise known as working through your imposter syndrome. This is the art-it-out, art-it-in method in action, which was described in the Intro to Art Therapy section.

- **Enhancing the purpose or spirit of what you are trying to accomplish.** Art therapy reflects back to you the energy of what you wish to create. This makes your intentions and goals more tangible.

- **Embodying your beliefs and connecting to the heart of what drives you.** By honoring what you wish to bring to life, art therapy helps you recognize when you're "walking the walk, and talking the talk". This is a true confidence booster!

THE POWER OF SIMPLICITY.
AND ENJOY THIS WONDERFUL NATURAL RESOURCE WE HAVE.
Planning Ahead
MAKE A WISH
FOR ALL THE WAYS YOU PLAY
ver
w leaf
of experience
EBB FLOW
THE BEAUTIFUL WAY TO SAVE ENERGY
Healing Cor
Magic sometimes requires a little push
When Love Comes
Joy
There are days when everything just flows.
cover rich spices
t recipes
d one another
CURIOUS PEOPLE
MAXWELL HOUSE
TEARS OF FREEDOM
Lon
a he
happ
Keepers
OF THE
flame
Peace
Discover the Secrets
WALK THE TALK
Take it Outside
daily dose
Stay Connected
yes
FUEL
INTUITIVE
Brighten your worldview
I Work for Earth
life lessons
CIVIL R 56
BOOST YOUR ENERGY
Miracle ELEMENT
Your Body Ritual

SPIRIT LOVE
PROMPTS

Let's nurture your relationship.

Your spirit reflects your unique radiance, the inner light that guides you.

Your spirit, however you personally define it, is tested by critical life moments, where it feels like everything has changed. You question everything you thought you knew to be true.

Yet, your relationship with your spirit benefits from facing these dark nights of the soul. It heals and grows by re-assessing your belief system. This helps you recognize the limiting beliefs that restrict your ability to feel, embrace, and share the power of self-love.

These tests of faith help you to see how strong you are without having to deny what hurts. You see how capable you are when the unexpected happens. You discover how amazing you truly are, faults and all.

When you foster self-love and acceptance through the relationship with your spirit, you tap into the sacred source of your resilience. When you embody the light at the end of the tunnel within yourself, it cannot be extinguished. May the following prompts help you feel this possibility.

SHOW IT THROUGH ART

Imagine that this song was written in your honor. Feel how the words, the rhythm, the beat moves your spirit. Feel your spirit soar and glow.

Prompt 12: Consider what it would feel like if your spirit is a ball of light that wants to play with you. Imagine that you are playing with this ball

like a juggler. Toss it up in the air, let it roll from one arm to the other.
As you play, you feel joy, love, and peace glowing within your heart.

into the warmth of your spirit's light. Feel safe, seen, and heard. Notice how this strengthens the bond and love between you and your spirit.

SHOW IT THROUGH ART

These moves that say YES to life, YES to yourself, YES to the love your spirit has for you. Feel your glow grow.

SHOW IT THROUGH ART

See how the leaves of your flower sustain your spirit's life force. Feel the softness of the petals, reflecting the loving kindness of your spirit.

6 Ways to Use Art Therapy as Emotional First Aid

How many times have you experienced feelings showing up when support isn't available, like in the middle of the night? This first aid kit is meant to support you through the storm.

- **#1 Meditative Art Process.** Take a break by immersing yourself in the creative process. First, find a focus for drawing, like a potted plant. Then do your best to try and replicate it. Or, put on a song and paint what the music sounds like to you.

- **#2 Tell the Story of What's Happening Inside.** Whether it's a memory, stress from the present moment, a belief that is creating anxiety, etc., illustrate what's coming up for you related to this distress. Let the paper or canvas hold onto it for you.

- **#3 Visual Journaling for Clarity.** Use the combination of art and writing to express what feels confusing. Tell the story of what you're grappling with through color, shape, and form This can help you calm your nervous system, increase self-awareness and understanding, and help you discover creative solutions.

6 Ways to Use Art Therapy as Emotional First Aid

- **#4 Adult Coloring Books.** This form of structured art making can help you feel more grounded and safe. Life might not feel predictable, but the coloring page you are working with will help you feel more contained because all you need to do is add color to bring it to life.

- **#5 Refocus Your Brain with Crafts.** knitting, crochetting, and other craft activities can give your brain a break by refocusing it on something that requires concentration for construction.

- **#6 Visualization.** Take yourself mentally to a place that you love. Engage your senses to further enhance the relaxation this brings. What do you see, smell, hear, taste, and/or touch when you are there? How can you reflect that through art?

Weathering the storms of life is not easy. The good news is that art therapy and writing are always available, 24 hours a day, 7 days a week. When I was going through chemotherapy, I always brought my pre-packed canvas tote with supplies. May these ideas serve you well.

SELF LOVE
PROMPTS

Let's nurture your relationship.

Your self, your identity, evolves throughout your entire life. The key is to show up for the process.

One lesson life teaches us is that we're here to learn how to adapt and change. Self-love provides a lens of compassion that can transform how you heal and grow. This softens tendencies that can block progress, and can help you embrace your whole self.

Self-acceptance is the key to unlocking your potential. Everyone is a work in progress. Your self is the center that holds your story and connects your body, mind, and spirit. This helps you listen to your wisdom and find meaning.

By approaching healing and growth with curiosity and creativity, you become flexible and open to what's possible, right here, right now. This creates a sense of freedom inside your body, mind, spirit, and self.

When you foster self-love and acceptance through your relationship with your identity, you affirm that you're worthy of your time and energy. You become clear about your needs, boundaries, and direction in life. May the following prompts help you feel this possibility.

See yourself snuggling with them and feel their beloved, sacred comfort fill you up. Notice how this grows your self-love glow.

SHOW IT THROUGH ART

Repeat their words until you feel your self-love is fully replenished by their affection for you.

evolve and grow through your life. Your branches reflect what matters most to you. Trust that you live as a testimony to the power of love.

SHOW IT THROUGH ART

the materials you need, ones that hold the magic of self -love.
Construct your nest and rest until you're filled with their energy.

Prompt 20: Repeat, out loud or in your head, the following: "I give myself permission to be who I am today. I allow myself to enjoy who

I am. I love myself fully and completely. I am enough." Experience the power of acceptance and how it helps you grow your self-love glow.

The saying goes that endings are beginnings...

You've done it! You're here and you're on the precipice of your next chapter.

All too often, we don't take the time to truly celebrate our accomplishments. This is your invitation to take a moment and reflect upon where your self-love journey has taken you. Do you:

- Recall what it was like to discover *Grow Your Glow*?
- Remember how it felt to be courageous enough to embark upon your journey?
- Looking back, what were your expectations of how it would feel vs. what you experienced?
- Do you remember the moment in which art and writing to grow your glow began to feel like second nature?
- How has your relationship with your body, mind, spirit, and self evolved as you committed to growing your glow?

You've found new ways of harnessing your creativity to learn, heal, and grow. These skills will be with you always and will continue to serve you as you move forward.

The best part of learning something new, in my humble opinion, is figuring out how to put your unique twist on it! I hope you reach out to me and share your experience and evolution.

As I say each week on my radio show: until we meet again, I invite you to spark your curiosity and tune into your creativity, so you can live radiantly.

Until we meet again,

Stephanie

PS. Let's stay in touch! To connect with me, visit stephaniemcleodestevez.com or use this QR code.

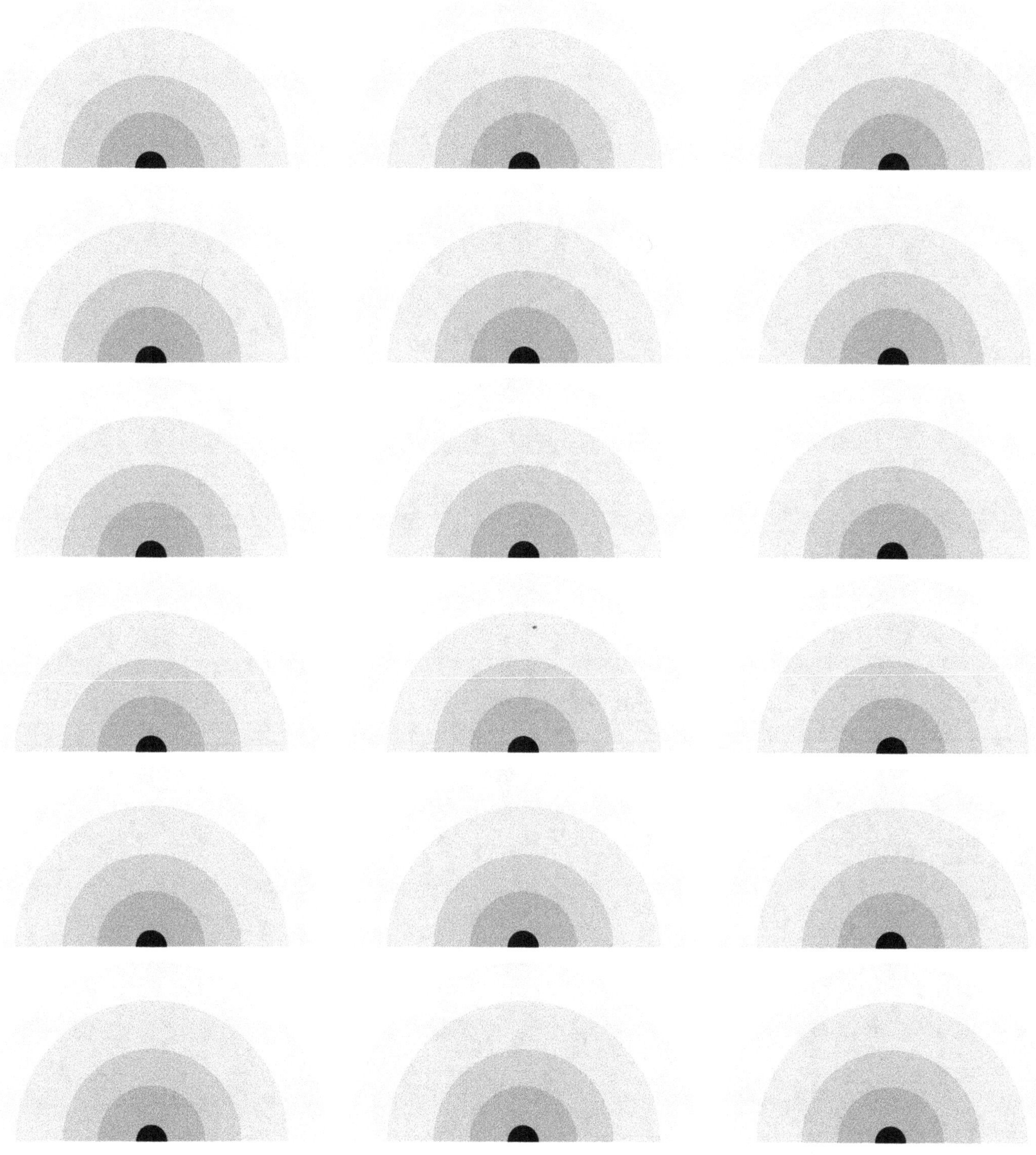

www.ingramcontent.com/pod-product-compliance
Lightning Source LLC
Chambersburg PA
CBHW060217120726
48004CB00008B/1850